Twenty-One Poems

Kimberly Hansen

BookLeaf
Publishing

India | USA | UK

Made with ❤ on the BookLeaf Publishing Platform
www.bookleafpub.in
www.bookleafpub.com

Dedication

To my sister Sadie who loves writing so much, and my sister Courtney who joined me on this Challenge.

Preface

Near the beginning of October, I saw this writing
challenge in my Instagram feed from BookLeaf
Publishing. The challenge was to write a poem daily for
21 days, and then they would turn it into my own poetry
book. At the beginning of the year, I had set a new year's
resolution to write and publish a book by the end of
2024. Though I had begun researching and taking notes
for a novel which I would like to write, I hadn't gotten
very far and realized I wouldn't be able to do it this year,
not justly to the story. This poetry challenge seemed
perfect and attainable. I've written quite a bit of poetry,
and I have thought of creating a book of my poetry
before. Though I could submit poems I had already
written, I decided to write all twenty-one poems new for
this book. I did start a little earlier than the challenge
and so the poems were not all written one a day for
Twenty-one days, but they were written between the
twelfth of October and the 10th of November 2024.

Acknowledgements

Thank you to BookLeaf Publishing and their team for issuing this writing challenge and making this possible.

1. Little Bird

Light feet of a little bird
Dance upon the ground.
It flits it wings, and spreads them wide,
And spins itself around.

Its talons leave such little marks
And writing on the land.
Calligraphy, and poetry
Impressed upon the sand.

Written words that can't be spoke,
But only sung and played.
The feeling written on the earth
Which glowed upon its face.

It shuffles with its little claws,
And it scuttles 'round and 'round.
And with its dance it sings its song,
A lovely, joyful sound.

If you look just close enough,
You might just glimpse a part
Of the joy and love a little bird
Was feeling in its heart.

2. Dozing Off

Sleep fills my eyes,
And my eyelids slowly close.
I drift through thoughts and memories
As I drift into a doze.

I wander in a warping time,
And a wonky colored setting.
The sea is red, and the sky is orange,
And I wonder what I'm forgetting.

Then the setting 'round me shifts
And doesn't make full sense,
But I don't know why it doesn't yet.
The fog ...of my brain ...is dense.

...

3. The Wind as He Whistles

The wind, he whistled as he ran
And rustled all the leaves.
The branches waved as he passed by
And enjoyed the lovely breeze.

He took a breath and then exhaled,
The blades of grass they bowed.
He slowed his pace and wiped his face,
His feet back on the ground.

He strolled into the meadow clear
And laid among the flowers.
He rested as he watched the clouds
And thought for many hours.

Swiftly he was up once more
And began to run again,
For the clouds had waited all this time
As he rested in the glen.

High into the sky they went
And far across the trees,
Through the valleys and over hills,
Until they came to the sea.

"Wait here a moment," he said to the clouds,
Then he wandered far to the right,
And he ran past a boy and his father
So that they could fly their kite.

A smile turned up upon his face
As he carried the boy's kite high,
And saw the joy upon the boy's face
As his kite flew up in the sky.

Then he ran the length of the beach
And danced with all the seagulls.
As they floated on his gentle breeze
He waved to all the people.

People on the little sail boats
And the people on land,
To each he stopped and looked upon,
And gave a helping hand.

Then he whistled, "so long, my friends,"
Looking back to the boy and the father
"Keep coming back, I'll be around!"
Then he smiled as the boy stood taller.

"We're on our way!" he whistled loud
Grabbing hold of all the clouds' reins,
Then ran them out over the open sea
As it neared the end of the day.

4. Playing Among the Pines

Deep in the forest
Among the deep green pines,
A little boy played with the twigs
And gave no thought to time.

He built a little wooden wall
Around a small twig cabin,
Then he set a guard about,
So nothing bad would happen.

The guard he set was made of rocks,
His clothes were made of leaves.
He held a wooden sword in hand
To defend the home from thieves.

He guards the home from danger.
He guards the home from harm,
When the little boy who built the home
Raises the alarm.

5. The War

Sorrow fills my heart
As another friend is lost.
This journey just begun,
But already such a cost.

Though many times I'm injured,
My friends have saved my life,
Yet somehow, I can't save them
Amidst the raging fight.

Another one has fallen
In honor, oh the brave.
How much can my heart wounded be?
It weeps in so much pain.

Still, we journey ever on.
There's danger still ahead,
But staying here would not be safe.
To stay we'd join the dead.

Danger up ahead of us,
And danger at our backs,
But moving forward gives us hope,
Which wallowing sorrow lacks.

Another step, we heave ahead,
Press forward on this quest.
When we find a little sacred place
We take a watchful rest.

Our tummies fed, our minds awake,
We pack our bags to go.
This company and restful place
Has soothed a hurting soul.

The laughs of those who still remain,
The strength of caring men,
Has given me the strength I need
To face the world again.

Gratefully we wander on.
Though perilous the path,
We do not face our fears alone,
Or all of dangers rath.

- - Part 2 - -

The war we're in still rages on.
We mustn't quit the fight,
Or all the things for which we care
Be lost in blackened night.

Keep trudging on through mud and moss;
Keep tramping through the snow.
Whatever forces push you back,
Be brave, be true, be bold

Steady arms are at your side
To lend you helping hands.
They bear you up, just keep your faith
And forever you will stand.

Give help to those who stand in need,
And hold your standards high.
When all seems lost, don't turn away,
Hold up your Savior's light.

He'll comfort you, he'll strengthen you,
You needn't stand in fear.
He will strengthen you with love,
So keep him always near.

He is the one who gives us peace.
He calms the stormy sea.
He gives us grace and gives us rest.
To him I'll bend my knee.

With him we'll win this raging war.
Through him we overcome.
All trials, burden, sorrows, pains,
Are covered by the Son.

6. The Wind's cry

The wind is at my back;
I hear her echoed cries.
She whistles her remorse;
Her tears fall from the sky.

Her tears of sorrow sting me
As they pelt into my skin.
Her sorrow rages through the air
And clouds, the skylights dim.

Her sorrow's strong, her cry is loud,
And she grasps me in her hand.
I have no wings to soar the sky,
But she picked me off the land.

"Help me, please!" I heard her cry.
In the clouds I saw her face.
She didn't want to cause me harm,
But remove this bitter taste.

"What can I do to ease your pain
And heal your tattered heart?
I'm just a girl, I'm just so small.
How can I even start?"

"Nature's dying", she said to me
As she gasped in her teary storm,
"And man cares not though we care for him
Contention an evil form.

Hate has caused so much despair;
Indifference signs defeat.
Take up love, a breath of air,
And sing love's trumpet sweet.

Call to all the caring men,
The men who love their kin.
Fight with all the love you have,
Love's the only way to win.

The world's in turmoil, can't you see?
So please before time's gone.
Share the love we have for you
And warm the breaking dawn.

7. Early Snow Fall

I'm sad for the trees,
For they have not yet lost their leaves,
So they bear a heavy load.

Weighed down by the snow,
Last night in a sudden storm blown,
And the colors were buried in white.

Six inches of wet
On the branches thick set,
And the trees arms drooped low to the ground.

Their backs were all spent,
Nearly torn down and rent,
I feared they would snap and fall down.

To see the dear trees
Fall down to their knees
Hurt my heart with a worry and woe.

Now there are scars
That run down their bark,
From weight of the too early snow.

8. Early Morning Journey

The night is old,
The day is young,
The day has only just begun.

Not for all,
For they still sleep
Bundled up in safety's keep.

The air is chill
And soon I leave,
Off to do important things.

I'm on my way,
The sky still dark,
Yet on my journey I embark.

I've dressed me warm
In many clothes
To keep from chilling to the bones.

I meet with friends
To share this trip;
A cup of cocoa we all sip.

The air is cold;
The ground is white.
What a splendid, lovely sight.

Through the trees
We wander far,
Gone on foot, not in a car.

Wandered off
The beaten trail,
We stride along a winter gale.

There we walk
Through fallen snow,
Until at dusk we come back home.

9. I Did Not Know I Loved Him

Once when I was young
I loved someone...
A dear friend who meant so much to me,
Yet I did not know I loved him.
I avoided the thought,
Though somewhere was besought:
"Who do you love?"
The question stirred.
"And who loves you?"
I also heard.
"Well... I know not.
And who asks me so?
Is this my heart that wants to know?"
Yes, ... I'm sure it is.
My heart it longs for these questions cured,
And so, I opened up to reflection -
Who I loved,
And who loved me;
And to my mind one face appeared,
Though I knew not through all these years
That his face kept on the shelf of my mind
In a picture frame for all this time.

His gentle smile,
His caring eyes,
And I remembered he was oh so kind.
Once so close,
But now so far,
Yet love holds on
Within one's heart.
I do not know
Where has he gone,
And this new thought I dwell upon.
Once our lives
Were intertwined,
As if I was his
And he was mine.
Yet just a child
Both we were,
With little thought of life did stir
Beyond those years of bliss and fun,
But now since all those years are done
Our lives moved on.
We moved away,
And now on this such random day
I wonder deep within my heart
In which direction did he depart?
For once again to see his face
Would surely make my heart to race.
Yet he bestills a gentle calm,

And I wish I were within his arms.
If I but knew before this day
That I had loved him in this way,
Would we have paths too different tread
If we had spoke the love unsaid?
Has his heart whispered him the same?
And spoke so suddenly my name?
Does his mind have a shelf for me
That keeps my face for him to see?
When his heart whispers,
"Who do you love?
And who loves you?"
Oh, I wish that I but knew.

10. Heart and Mind

I am tired,
My body fatigued.
Breathing is heavy.
My heart works fast,
And yet it's not enough.
The world around me blurs.
It spins, and then it fades.

I wake to a ray of light shining in through the window.
My head throbs.
I try to remember where I am
And how I got here.
Then I remember the dizziness,
The heaviness, and the fatigue as I start to pick myself
up.
I'm reminded of it all, as my stiff, heavy muscles express
their depression to me?
How long has this lasted?
When did it come on?
Was I blind to it until it hit me in the back of the head
and knocked me out cold?
There, the cold.
I then realized my shivering and my goosebumps.
At this, my teeth started chattering.

Had I been so cold before this thought?
Where has my mind been to not have noticed my aching
body?
Or perhaps I should ask where has my heart been?
My heart in charge of feeling.
Have they not been speaking to one another?
Oh, the pains of a rebellious heart and a rebellious mind,
Of a chasm that divides them in two
And a wall that keeps them from speaking.
Two who are meant to be one,
And yet have become disgruntled foreigners one to
another.
Where has your marriage gone, Reason and Feeling?
Have you truly forsaken each other?
Your neglectfulness leaves you both broken and weak.
My mind filled with a fog and a forgetfulness.
To leave one's heart does not enhance the mind,
But blinds it and makes it naive and ignorant,
A tyrant to itself.
My heart aches and tires
Carrying such a heavy load on its own.
Too much to bear on a lonely, saddened back,
All the burdens of a million hurting souls.
Oh, heart why have you left reason?
Have you felt so many times unheard that you refused
any longer to speak?
What is your quarrel with reason?

Does reason not keep you from plunging too far into the abyss?
Does he not teach you how to have boundaries and how to take care of yourself?
Find remedy to your malfunction, heart and mind.
For without your unity
Surely each of you will perish.
And along with you,
All the parts of the body.
Without you both
No part can fill its purpose,
No instrument can play its song,
For all just rots away and leaves this life a tattered wasteland.

11. The End

The iron tool is rusted.
The flesh, it all decays.
The strings which once were splendid
Break with one last sorrow's twang.

The twang of strings when bursting
Breaks the lullaby of night.
Then swollen muscles burn with heat,
Bursting seams with anger's knife.

The heated burning frenzy
Leaves a poison in the veins
That travels every single course,
Filling body ripe with pain.

Then within you eats the fire
All of life that's left and raw,
Until there's nothing left at all,
Consumed like burning straw.

All you once did hold so close
The moth does now corrupt,
And the heated furnace burns away
At the world's last evening sup.

12. In the Valleys

Fountains spring up in the valleys.
The sky is bright and vast,
Deep clouds are lit like fires,
And leave no shadows cast.

Walls of rock form mountains,
The caves of which make homes
For many of the creatures
Which 'round this valley roam.

Rivers flow to lake beds;
Deep water fills the holes
Where everything is gathered
To drink from nature's bowl.

Crowded on the lakeside
The creatures do not stay.
Not always do they get along,
Some predators, some prey.

A campsite in the forest,
A strange man in his bed
Among the needles of the pines,
He lays his tired head.

This man is on a journey
Where no one really knows,
Except the one who shows the way
Through rain, through sun, through snow.

13. What Are the Clouds?

What are the clouds
That float above our heads?
That give us rain
And water our garden beds?

So soft, so light,
Then dark and heavy.
I stare up at the clouds
So happily, contently.

So many colors I see in them.
They truly paint the sky
With soft strokes and feathered pillows,
Rising up to greater heights.

If I could just lay my head upon them
And drift in the currents of the air
As if I was on a mattress
Floating down a tranquil river,

But I roll to my tummy
And look down to the earth
And see the little sheep
And the trees and all the dirt.

Now the earth is what I stare at
As I lay up in the sky.
How did I get up here?
Through the air I glide.

I dreamt that I was up here,
Then suddenly I was
Upon the pillows in the sky,
And dreaming made it thus.

14. The Earth Whispers to Me

The earth whispers to me,
It calls me by my name.
She sends her beauty to my heart,
And to her heart I came.

Her heart is made of warmth.
She presents me with her ore
With all her lovely precious stones,
She said to me, "they're yours.

They're here to show you beauty.
They're here to give you wealth,
But not just wealth of money,
But of knowledge of myself.

I'm here to serve for lifetimes.
I'm here so you can live,
Experience so many things,
The path to growth I give.

Feed yourself with knowledge,
With learning, and with love
As you feel the earth beneath your feet,
You who came from up above.

Your spirit came from heaven
To your body here on earth.
Your little vessel made of clay
Yet, how much more it's worth.

One day your dust returns to me,
But I know you'll live again,
For the one who created both of us
Will raise you up again."

15. Memory

Memory.
I remember you holding me,
Remember sitting on your lap.
I remember dancing round
And while I danced you clapped.
I remember you read to me
As I laid upon my bed,
And as I fell asleep
You whispered, and you said,
"Good night,
I love you.
Sleep well my little child.
I'll hum for you a little tune
and stay with you a while.
When morning breaks
I'll be right here
to hold you in my arms,
And let you know I love you
As I keep you safe from harm.
We'll eat pancakes for breakfast.
Lunch, a picnic in the park.
Tomorrow we can dance and play
Until the night gets dark."

16. If I Could Comfort You

Oh, if I could comfort you,
If I could give you joy
When your heart is filled with sorrow
Like a cold and empty void.

If I could stop your weeping,
If I could wipe away your tears,
If I could fill your heart with peace
That lasts for all the years.

I wish that you were happy.
I wish that you had joy.
I won't leave you to fight alone
When your peace has been destroyed.

Come, let me sit beside you.
Lay your head upon my chest.
Breathe deep and fill your lungs with air.
Breathe deep and take a rest.

My arm is wrapped around you;
I shield you from this storm
As you sit with me and rest your soul
From this great and heavy war.

17. When the Earth Shakes

When the earth shakes
And the mountains tumble
And the valleys fill with sand,
Reach up,
I'm reaching out for you,
Reach up and take my hand.

When the night comes
And the sky is dark
And night will not depart,
Look up,
I shine a light for you,
Look up and see the stars.

When storms arise
And waters flood
And there's chaos all around,
Be still,
I calm this storm for you,
Be still, know you are found.

18. Choose the Things That Make You Sing

Seldom does the hour come
When all is set and all is done.
Most of time it's disarray,
And lots of things to fill the day.

Choice is set before our sight
To choose which choice is better right.
There is not time for everything,
So, choose the things that make you sing.

19. Our Woven Thread

When all is still
And all is dead,
Keep what's loved
In a woven thread;
And wrap it round
My tattered corps,
Words unsaid
In a throat so hoarse.
Tears and sobs
Have rubbed it raw
From the anguish
In your heart it gnaws,
But wrap me in this
Precious cloak,
Remember life
A breath awoke.
I'll remember
As I'm wrapped in love,
And carry your heart
To the heavens above.
I'll shower you with blessings
Too many to count.
Keep your faith.
Let go of your doubt.

We are knit together;
With love's thread we are made,
Our tapestry woven,
Never to fade.

20. The Mystic of the Old

Life is beautiful.
Reflecting on the history of the earth and her people
And the magic of the myths and legends.
The inspiration and wonder that come from those things
of the past.
The old inspires and teaches the new.
We dig to discover.
We dig to learn.
We dig to uncover,
The secrets of the earth.
She holds so many stories, her pages, the earth,
Each layer like an onion telling stories in the dirt.
We look at what's around us,
What was build up in the past.
But now it all is weathered,
Mostly gone, but we make it last.
We hold on to the value
Of the simple dirty finds
That tell of people long ago
Before our modern time.
There's something in the oldness
That stirs this gentle heart,
And shows the beauty of this life
Which each of us take part.

I find that I'm connected
To the stories and the tales.
The mystic gives me peace and awe
And fills my learning sails.
The light it bids me forward,
And curious I come.
With open mind, loving earth and man
I listen for what's been sung.
Sung by the birds that have sat in these trees,
Of the winds that have sewn all these plants,
Of the water that's ebbed and once again flowed,
And of man who sings to life's dance.
The colors are spun as we dance through the days.
The shapes become different and new.
New knowledge, new sight, new experience displayed
But it's all from the old, weathered hues.
Once they were vibrant
And then they did fade,
But now they are vibrant once more
As they're added to the fabric and the dance they create
Of the person who dances this floor.

21. I Saw You
In the Meadow

I saw you in the meadow.
There.
Sitting on a rock
Waiting for something new,
Playing your little lute.
Your body swayed to rhythm,
Your feet tapped on the ground,
My stomach filled with butterflies
When I heard that sweet, soft sound.
Your melody played my eardrums,
And your beauty filled my eyes.
Your presence flooded over me,
And washed all hope of my disguise.
I found I wandered from the edge
Of the clearing where I stood,
And couldn't help but come to you,
And know you if I could.
Your rhythm was my heartbeat;
Your singing made me light.
Courage let me take your hand,
And then my heart took flight.
We danced around the meadow.

There.
In the sunlight we performed.
You for me and I for you,
My love for you confirmed.
I know you in your music.
I know you in your dance.
I know the way you look at me.
That moment,
What a joyful circumstance.